SUPER
SOCIAL STUDIES
INFOGRAPHICS

US HISTORY THROUGH INFOGRAPHICS

Karen Latchana Kenney

graphics by
Laura Westlund

Lerner Publications Company
Minneapolis

Lerner Publications Company
A division of Lerner Publishing Group, Inc.
241 First Avenue North
Minneapolis, MN 55401 USA

For reading levels and more information, look up this title at www.lernerbooks.com.

Main text set in Univers LT Std 12/15.
Typeface provided by Adobe Systems.

Library of Congress Cataloging-in-Publication Data

Kenney, Karen Latchana.
    US history through infographics / by Karen Latchana Kenney; illustrated by Laura Westlund
        pages cm. — (Super social studies infographics)
    Includes index.
    ISBN 978–1–4677–3459–2 (lib. bdg. : alk. paper)
    ISBN 978–1–4677–4749–3 (eBook)
    1. United States—History—Juvenile literature. I. Title.
E178.3.K35 2015
973—dc23   2013041244

Manufactured in the United States of America
1 – PC – 7/15/14

CONTENTS

BACK IN TIME

Ready to test your US history knowledge? Take this quiz.

1. Do you wonder how long your family has lived in America?

2. Have you thought about who lived in your state before you?

3. Ever think about how you might have had a British accent instead of an American one?

4. Do you think about how hard it was for astronauts to reach the moon?

Did you answer yes to any of those questions?

CONGRATULATIONS!

You've got what it takes to become a first-rate historian. You can go back in time just by studying a country's history. The past is full of drama and danger—from important battles to amazing Americans. Historians use charts, graphs, and other infographics to make sense of these events and the people who shaped them. You can use these tools too! Let's learn about some incredible events from the history of the United States.

MOUND BUILDERS

American Indians lived off the North American land long before
Europeans came. Some of the earliest cultures were the Mound
Builders. The Adena people were the first Mound Builders. They
lived in the Ohio River valley from 1,000 BCE to 1 BCE. This culture
left behind large burial mounds. These mounds and the items found
inside tell us clues about the people who built them.

The largest Adena mound is the Grave Creek Mound in West Virginia.
It was built from 250 BCE to 150 BCE. Here's a look at the mound,
what was found inside, and what it tells us about the Adena people:

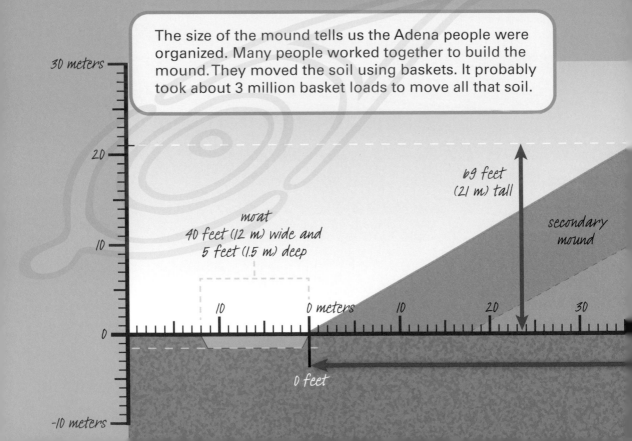

The size of the mound tells us the Adena people were
organized. Many people worked together to build the
mound. They moved the soil using baskets. It probably
took about 3 million basket loads to move all that soil.

30 meters

20

10

0

-10 meters

moat
40 feet (12 m) wide and
5 feet (1.5 m) deep

10   0 meters   10   20   30

0 feet

69 feet
(21 m) tall

secondary
mound

HOME TO THE ADENA

The Adena people lived in the Ohio River valley. This area includes parts of modern Ohio, West Virginia, Kentucky, and Indiana.

The Adena people were skilled at making fine crafts. They made jewelry and weapons using different materials. Many artifacts were found in the upper vault of the Grave Creek Mound.

1,700 bone and shell beads

five copper bracelets

neck jewelry

pieces of mica (a shiny type of rock)

a small rock with writing on it

upper vault contained one person and a variety of fine craft artifacts

Multiple burials suggest that the mound took years to build.

original mound

50   60   70   80   90 meters   10

GROUND LEVEL

lower vault contained two people and 650 shell beads

295 feet (90 m) wide at the base

THE NEW WORLD

European explorers found North America by accident. They were trying to get to Asia. Explorers went on sea voyages to find the fastest routes. But they bumped into an unfamiliar land on the way.

Soon explorers realized North America was a huge continent. They called it the New World. More and more explorers came. They claimed the land and its resources for their home countries.

1603 and 1608–1609: **Samuel de Champlain** searched for places to build a French settlement. He also made maps of explored areas.

1609

1603

1562: **Jean Ribault** wanted to start a French colony in Florida.

North America

1519–1521: **Hernán Cortés** searched for gold and silver mines.

1513: **Juan Ponce de León** hoped to find gold.

1497: **John Cabot** wanted to find goods to trade and explore unknown areas.

1524: **Giovanni da Verrazano** looked for a route around North America to India.

1609: **Henry Hudson** looked for a route to the Pacific Ocean through the Arctic.

Champlain: 1608

1492 and 1493: **Christopher Columbus** searched for a route to Asia. He hoped to find pearls, gold, spices, and other riches.

England

Holland

France

Spain

Africa

The Explorers and Their Countries

Spain:
   Columbus
   Ponce de León
   Cortés

Holland:
   Hudson

France:
   Verrazano
   Ribault
   Champlain

England:
   Cabot

Routes shown are estimates based on available historical sources.

STARTING A COLONY

Starting a colony in the New World was hard. Plans went into action years before any journeys began. To start a colony, people needed ships, supplies, and plenty of people. Colonists took a long journey across the Atlantic Ocean. Many challenges awaited. To survive, colonists had to be prepared.

William Penn planned for years. In 1682, his vision became a reality. His ships brought thousands of Europeans to the colony of Pennsylvania. There they would be able to freely practice their Quaker religion. Here's how Penn made it happen:

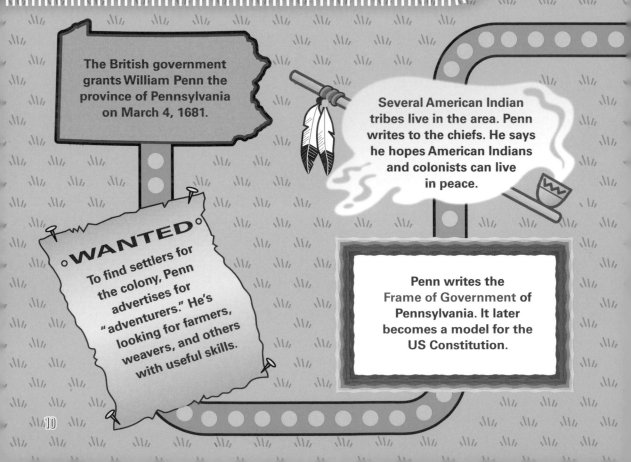

New World

The British government grants William Penn the province of Pennsylvania on March 4, 1681.

Several American Indian tribes live in the area. Penn writes to the chiefs. He says he hopes American Indians and colonists can live in peace.

WANTED
To find settlers for the colony, Penn advertises for "adventurers." He's looking for farmers, weavers, and others with useful skills.

Penn writes the Frame of Government of Pennsylvania. It later becomes a model for the US Constitution.

or Bust

Smallpox spreads on the ship. Nearly one-third of the passengers die.

He leaves England in August 1682. About 100 passengers sail with him on the ship *Welcome*.

The *Welcome* arrives at New Castle (now Delaware) on October 27, 1682.

Colonists elect representatives for their new government.

Penn buys more land from the Lenni-Lenape peoples. Within a year, the colonists start 300 farms in Pennsylvania.

By 1699, the colony is thriving. It exports many goods, including lumber, furs, iron, and copper. The population is growing.

AMERICAN INDIAN POPULATIONS

When colonists arrived in North America, they brought diseases that American Indians had never had before. Between illness and clashes with colonists, American Indian populations shrank. Here's what happened to the Lenni-Lenape:

20,0000

1600: More than 20,000 Lenni-Lenape live in Pennsylvania, New Jersey, and New York.

1682: Only about 4,000 Lenni-Lenape are left by the time William Penn arrives.

4,000

11

SLAVE TRADE

Crops were the new gold in colonial America. Colonists knew they could get rich farming. But they needed workers to tend crops. Finding cheap labor was a problem. Slavery was the solution for many southern plantation owners. During the 1600s and the 1700s, hundreds of thousands of Africans were kidnapped, brought to the colonies, and sold as slaves. These people were treated as property. They were part of a system called the triangle trade. Here is how the process worked:

Traders left Europe in slave ships loaded with goods. Most traders sailed from Portugal, Spain, Britain, France, Denmark, Sweden, and the Netherlands.

Traders sold slaves to planters or slave dealers. Slaves were separated from their families and forced to work for their new owners. Traders bought goods Europeans wanted. Then the traders returned to Europe to sell their goods.

sugarcane

rice

cotton

The Americas

Chesapeake

Carolinas/ Georgia

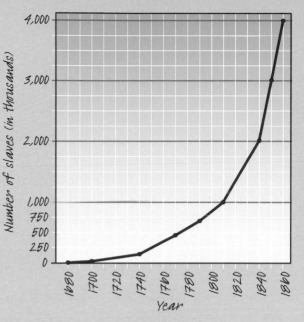

Slaves became a huge part of the population in colonial America. More and more slaves were brought to the colonies each year. And children of slaves became slaves too. Here's how the number of slaves grew over the decades.

ATLANTIC OCEAN

Traders traded their goods for African slaves. Hundreds of captured people were crammed into traders' ships. They sailed to the Americas.

Africa

THE ROAD TO INDEPENDENCE

British colonists in North America were tired of being told what to do by a king thousands of miles away. High and unfair taxes angered many colonists. Some wanted to break away from British rule and create a new nation. The road to independence was long and bumpy, but the 13 American colonies finally got there in 1783.

The British Parliament passes the **Stamp Act**. Colonists must pay a tax on every piece of paper they use. Angry colonists protest this tax.

1765

October 1768

British troops arrive in Boston. They are there to enforce British laws.

– July 1776 –
The Continental Congress adopts the **Declaration of Independence**.

1776

July

George Washington takes command of the American army.

December

1776

1777–1778

Washington's army crosses the Delaware River to launch a surprise attack on enemy troops. The **Battle of Trenton** is a much-needed victory for the colonists.

British troops take control of Philadelphia. But Americans win important victories at Saratoga. France enters the war by supporting the colonists.

Colonists at the Boston Tea Party protest British tea taxes. Protesters dump boxes of tea into the Boston Harbor.

December 1773

March 1774

Britain passes the Coercive Acts. These laws set harsh rules about trade in Boston. They also set up martial law.

The first Continental Congress meets in Philadelphia. Representatives from the colonies gather and discuss how to oppose Britain.

September 1774

A mob of colonists threatens some British troops. The troops kill four colonists. This event becomes known as the **Boston Massacre**.

March 1770

British troops march to Concord, Massachusetts. Their mission is to destroy weapons that the colonists are storing there. A small colonist militia fights off 700 British soldiers at Lexington and Concord.

April 1775

The first major battle occurs at **Bunker Hill**. The British win, but both sides suffer serious losses.

June 1775

October 1781
Together, American and French forces attack the British at the **Battle of Yorktown**. The British surrender.

MERGE

AMERICA

FRANCE

- SEPTEMBER -

BRITAIN SIGNS THE **TREATY OF PARIS**, RECOGNIZING AMERICA AS AN INDEPENDENT NATION.

-1783

GROWTH AND DISCOVERY

In 1803, the United States was getting crowded. European Americans wanted more land. So President Thomas Jefferson jumped at the chance to buy territory from France. Through the Louisiana Purchase, Jefferson instantly doubled the size of the United States.

But the newly bought territory wasn't empty. Many American Indian tribes lived there. Jefferson sent a group of explorers to learn more about these tribes and the land. The group was called the Corps of Discovery. Led by Meriwether Lewis and William Clark, the Corps spent more than two years exploring the Louisiana Territory. Take a look at the Corps' route—and just a few of the Indian peoples they met along the way.

November 1805: The Corps reaches the Pacific Ocean.

Clatsop

Nez Perce

SPANISH

Columbia Plateau

Northwest Coast

- ◎ Point of contact between the Corps and the tribes
- ← Corps of Discovery, route west
- → Corps of Discovery, route east
- ■ ■ ■ ➤ Lewis • • • • • ➤ Clark
- Louisiana Purchase
- – · – Current international borders
- – – – Current state borders

Crow

Blackfeet

Shoshone

Hidatsa

Mandan

Teton Sioux

Yankton Sioux

Missouri

Oto

May 1804:
Corps of Discovery enters Louisiana Territory.

St. Louis, Missouri

September 1806:
The Corps returns to St. Louis.

Great Basin

Each American Indian tribe has a distinct culture. But some tribes developed similar lifestyles and traditions based on the areas where they lived. Certain regions became home to related "culture groups" of Indian peoples. Notice the culture areas along the Corps' route.

Great Plains

TERRITORY

CONNECTED CULTURES

READY, SET, HOMESTEAD!

Thanks to the Louisiana Purchase, the United States had plenty of land. But most European Americans still lived along the East Coast. To encourage them to move west, the Homestead Act was passed in 1862. It gave free land to people who wanted to settle in the central United States. But settlers had to follow a few steps to get that land. Here's what they had to do:

Stay for five years. Settlers could not give up on their farms. They had to show they would put the land to good use. This meant dealing with intense blizzards and crop-eating insects.

Travel to the land. Settlers had to travel across rough land to get to their homesteads. They also had to buy and bring the supplies needed to get their farm started.

Grow crops. Settlers had to develop their land. They had to clear the land and plant and grow crops. It was extremely hard work.

Apply for land rights. Settlers first had to apply for the temporary right to use the land. After five years, they could apply for the title to the land. This would make them official owners.

Be the right age. The head of the household had to be at least 21 years old.

Be a citizen. The homesteader had to be a US citizen.

Build a house. Homesteaders had to build a 12- to 14-foot (3.7 to 4.3 m) house on the land. Lumber was hard to get, so many houses were made with sod.

THE BLOODIEST WAR

Slavery caused a split in the nation. Many people in the North wanted to end slavery. But the South relied on it. The issue helped spark the Civil War (1861–1865). Southern states tried to break away and form their own nation, the Confederate States of America. The North fought to keep the United States together. What followed was the bloodiest war in American history. Nearly 750,000 men died—around 2.5 percent of the US population at the time. Here are some of the war's major battles and the number of soldiers killed, captured, and wounded:

CONFEDERATE DEATHS

Confederate (Southern) victories

Union (Northern) victories

neither side could claim victory

Confederate casualties (per 1,000)

Union casualties (per 1,000)

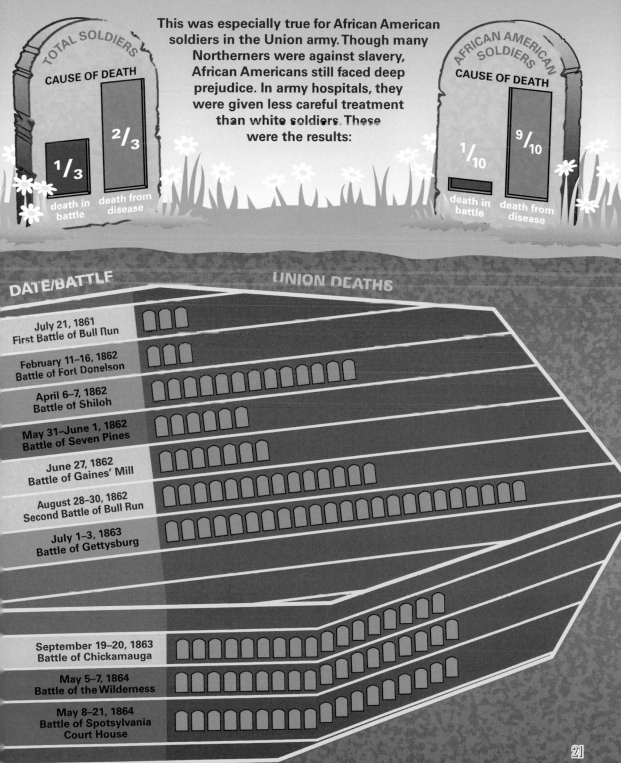

BEYOND THE BATTLES

Most soldiers who died in war weren't actually killed in battle. They died of disease.

This was especially true for African American soldiers in the Union army. Though many Northerners were against slavery, African Americans still faced deep prejudice. In army hospitals, they were given less careful treatment than white soldiers. These were the results:

TOTAL SOLDIERS
CAUSE OF DEATH

1/3 death in battle

2/3 death from disease

AFRICAN AMERICAN SOLDIERS
CAUSE OF DEATH

1/10 death in battle

9/10 death from disease

DATE/BATTLE — UNION DEATHS

July 21, 1861
First Battle of Bull Run

February 11–16, 1862
Battle of Fort Donelson

April 6–7, 1862
Battle of Shiloh

May 31–June 1, 1862
Battle of Seven Pines

June 27, 1862
Battle of Gaines' Mill

August 28–30, 1862
Second Battle of Bull Run

July 1–3, 1863
Battle of Gettysburg

September 19–20, 1863
Battle of Chickamauga

May 5–7, 1864
Battle of the Wilderness

May 8–21, 1864
Battle of Spotsylvania
Court House

21

NEW, BIG IDEAS

In the decades after the Civil War, America was in its golden age. Farming was out—industry was in. It was the time of new inventions, from the lightbulb to the gasoline engine to Coca-Cola. These inventions helped American businesses grow—and had a lasting impact on the way Americans lived.

The invention of the telephone was one especially important breakthrough. It dramatically changed the way we communicate. And it started a whole new industry.

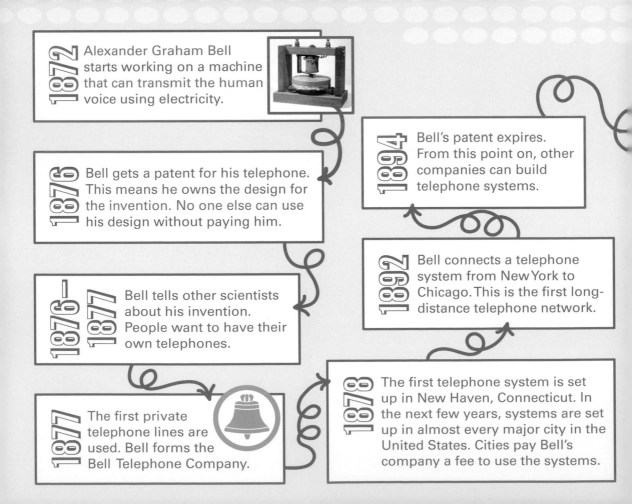

1872 Alexander Graham Bell starts working on a machine that can transmit the human voice using electricity.

1876 Bell gets a patent for his telephone. This means he owns the design for the invention. No one else can use his design without paying him.

1876–1877 Bell tells other scientists about his invention. People want to have their own telephones.

1877 The first private telephone lines are used. Bell forms the Bell Telephone Company.

1878 The first telephone system is set up in New Haven, Connecticut. In the next few years, systems are set up in almost every major city in the United States. Cities pay Bell's company a fee to use the systems.

1892 Bell connects a telephone system from New York to Chicago. This is the first long-distance telephone network.

1894 Bell's patent expires. From this point on, other companies can build telephone systems.

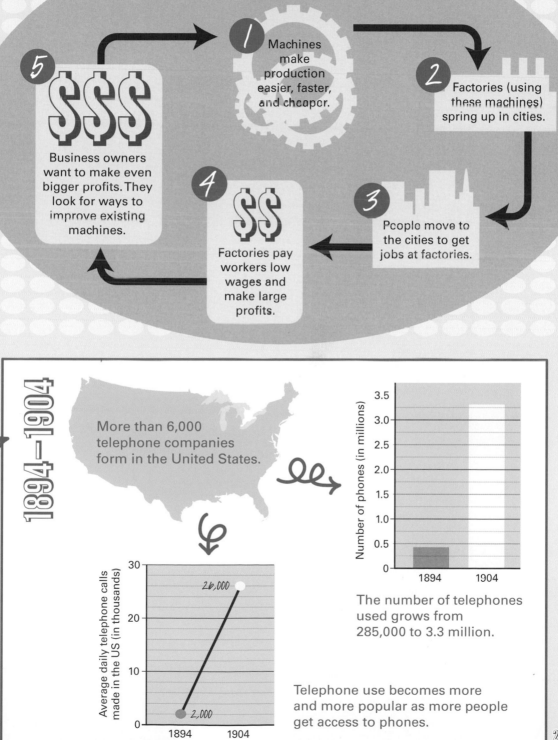

INDUSTRIALIZATION 101

1 Machines make production easier, faster, and cheaper.

2 Factories (using these machines) spring up in cities.

3 People move to the cities to get jobs at factories.

4 Factories pay workers low wages and make large profits.

5 Business owners want to make even bigger profits. They look for ways to improve existing machines.

1894–1904

More than 6,000 telephone companies form in the United States.

The number of telephones used grows from 285,000 to 3.3 million.

Number of phones (in millions) — 3.5, 3.0, 2.5, 2.0, 1.5, 1.0, 0.5, 0 — 1894, 1904

Average daily telephone calls made in the US (in thousands) — 30, 20, 10, 0 — 26,000 (1904), 2,000 (1894)

Telephone use becomes more and more popular as more people get access to phones.

WAVES OF PEOPLE

By the end of the 19th century, it seemed that *everybody* wanted to come to America. It was the land of opportunity. New fortunes could be made. Land could be bought cheaply or was even free. From the late 1800s to the early 1900s, more than 30 million immigrants arrived, mostly from Europe. They came in waves, with many people from one country arriving during certain periods.

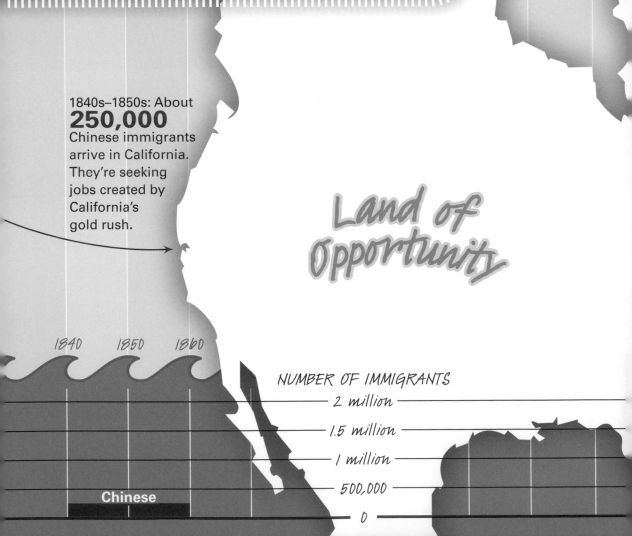

1840s–1850s: About **250,000** Chinese immigrants arrive in California. They're seeking jobs created by California's gold rush.

Land of Opportunity

1840   1850   1860

NUMBER OF IMMIGRANTS

2 million

1.5 million

1 million

500,000

0

Chinese

2 MILLION
1845–1855: About Irish immigrants arrive in the United States. Most come to escape poverty and hunger.

Ireland

Germany EUROPE

Italy

1 MILLION
1881–1885: About German immigrants arrive at the peak of the German wave. Many hope to escape poverty or find religious freedom.

2 MILLION
1881–1920: About eastern European Jews come to America at the peak of their immigration wave. Most come to escape prejudice and violence against Jews.

2 MILLION
1911–1920: About Italian immigrants arrive at the peak of their wave. Around this time, many poor people in Italy have lost their homes in natural disasters. They come to America to find jobs.

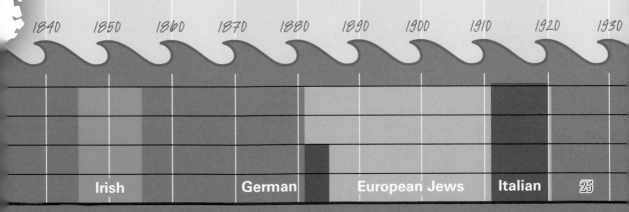

1840   1850   1860   1870   1880   1890   1900   1910   1920   1930

Irish   German   European Jews   Italian   25

ENEMY ALIENS

When Japan bombed Pearl Harbor during World War II (1939–1945), it became an enemy of the United States. Soon after, many Americans became suspicious of Japanese Americans who lived along the West Coast. These people had not done anything to hurt the United States. Many of them were US citizens. But they were seen as "enemy aliens." Some people thought Japanese Americans would become spies and traitors. Because of this fear, more than 120,000 Japanese Americans were forced to move to prison camps during the war. Here's where camps were located and how many people were sent there.

1,000 internees

Location of Camp	Number of Internees (rounded to the nearest thousand)
Tule Lake, California	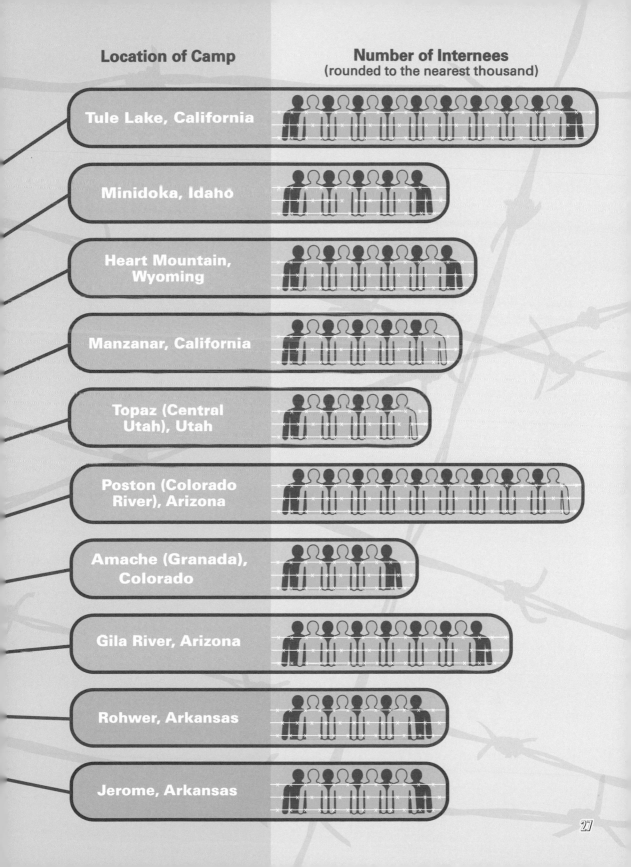
Minidoka, Idaho	
Heart Mountain, Wyoming	
Manzanar, California	
Topaz (Central Utah), Utah	
Poston (Colorado River), Arizona	
Amache (Granada), Colorado	
Gila River, Arizona	
Rohwer, Arkansas	
Jerome, Arkansas	

27

RACE TO SPACE

After World War II, the two biggest powers of the world were the United States and the Soviet Union (a group of 15 countries that included Russia). Each country wanted to prove its greatness. This led to the Space Race. Each country wanted to be the first to go into space. The ultimate destination was the moon. See how close the race actually was.

December 1968: *Apollo 8* is the first manned spacecraft to orbit the moon.

Apollo 8

Sputnik

October 1957: The Soviet Union starts the race by sending Sputnik into space. This is the first satellite to orbit Earth.

START

Explorer I

January 1958: The United States sends up its first satellite, Explorer I.

USA

USSR

9 Apollo 11

July 1969: On the *Apollo 11* space mission, the United States wins the race to the moon. Astronaut Neil Armstrong becomes the first man to walk on the moon.

FINISH

WINNER

USA

John Glenn 7

February 1962: Astronaut John Glenn is the first American to orbit Earth.

Alan Shepard 6

May 1961: Astronaut Alan Shepard is the first man from the United States to go into space. He does not orbit Earth.

3 Luna 2

September 1959: The Soviet Union launches the Luna 2 space probe. It is the first probe to reach the moon.

Yuri Gagarin 5

April 1961: Soviet astronaut Yuri Gagarin is the first man to orbit Earth.

4 Ham in Space

January 1961: Ham the chimpanzee is sent into space in the Mercury space capsule. He travels 155 miles (249 kilometers) in 16.5 minutes.

Glossary

CASUALTY: a person killed, wounded, or captured in an armed conflict

COLONY: an area controlled by a country that is usually far away

IMMIGRANT: a person who leaves one country to live in another

INDUSTRIALIZATION: making products by using machines in factories, or a group of businesses that make a particular product

INDUSTRY: making products by using machines in factories. *Industry* can also refer to a group of businesses that make a particular product.

ORBIT: to travel around a planet or an object in space, such as the moon

PARLIAMENT: a group of people elected to make laws in a country

PLANTATION: a large farm that grows crops such as cotton or coffee

POPULATION: all the people who live in a country or place

PROBE: a tool or machine used to explore something, such as the moon or space

QUAKER: a religion that values peace, is against war, and promotes simple services

RESOURCE: something valuable

SATELLITE: a spacecraft that is sent to orbit a planet or an object in space

TERRITORY: land that belongs to or is controlled by a government

TRAITOR: a person who aids the enemy of a country

Further Information

Figley, Marty Rhodes. *Who Was William Penn?* Minneapolis: Lerner Publications, 2012.
Discover more about this man who started the Pennsylvania colony in colonial America.

Gondosch, Linda. *How Did Tea and Taxes Spark a Revolution?* Minneapolis: Lerner Publications, 2011.
Have you wondered how the American Revolution started? Read this book to find the answers to your questions about the war.

Huey, Lois Miner. *Ick! Yuck! Eew! Our Gross American History.* Minneapolis: Millbrook Press, 2014.
Find out some disgusting yet true facts about American history in this book.

Kids.gov
http://kids.usa.gov/history/index.shtml
Check out this site to learn about different cultures in the United States, the US Constitution, and other interesting US history facts.

Lynette, Rachel. *The Louisiana Purchase.* New York: PowerKids Press, 2014.
Read about the land purchase that doubled the size of the United States.

Sandler, Martin W. *Imprisoned: The Betrayal of Japanese Americans during World War II.* New York: Walker, 2013.
Learn about the Japanese American prison camps of World War II.

TIME for Kids: "U.S.A. Timeline"
http://www.timeforkids.com/destination/usa/history-timeline
Visit this site to read a timeline on US history.

Waxman, Laura Hamilton. *Why Did the Pilgrims Come to the New World?* Minneapolis: Lerner Publications, 2011.
Discover why a group of English settlers traveled across the Atlantic to start a colony in the New World.

LERNER
e
SOURCE

Expand learning beyond the printed book. Download free, complementary educational resources for this book from our website, www.lerneresource.com.

Index